JUL 0 3 2017

LET'S READ

AV²
BY WEIGL™

ADDED VALUE • AUDIO VISUAL

Go to **www.av2books.com**, and enter this book's unique code.

BOOK CODE

Z 7 3 9 6 5 4

AV² by Weigl brings you media enhanced books that support active learning.

AV² provides enriched content that supplements and complements this book. Weigl's AV² books strive to create inspired learning and engage young minds in a total learning experience.

Your AV² Media Enhanced books come alive with...

Audio
Listen to sections of the book read aloud.

Video
Watch informative video clips.

Embedded Weblinks
Gain additional information for research.

Try This!
Complete activities and hands-on experiments.

Key Words
Study vocabulary, and complete a matching word activity.

Quizzes
Test your knowledge.

Slide Show
View images and captions, and prepare a presentation.

... and much, much more!

Published by AV² by Weigl
350 5th Avenue, 59th Floor
New York, NY 10118
Website: www.av2books.com

Library of Congress Cataloging-in-Publication Data

Carr, Aaron.
Jazz / Aaron Carr.
pages cm. -- (I love music)
Includes bibliographical references and index.
ISBN 978-1-4896-3581-5 (hard cover : alk. paper) -- ISBN 978-1-4896-3582-2 (soft cover : alk. paper) --
ISBN 978-1-4896-3583-9 (single user ebook) -- ISBN 978-1-4896-3584-6 (multi-user ebook)
1. Jazz--History and criticism--Juvenile literature. I. Title.
ML3506.C396 2015
781.6509--dc23
                                2015002872

Printed in the United States of America in Brainerd, Minnesota
1 2 3 4 5 6 7 8 9 0   19 18 17 16 15

072015
170415

Project Coordinator: Jared Siemens
Designer: Mandy Christiansen

The publisher acknowledges Alamy, Getty Images, and iStock as the primary image suppliers for this title.

Jazz

CONTENTS

I love music. Jazz is my favorite kind of music.

Jazz began in
the United States
in the early 1900s.

Jazz music came from Africa and Europe.

Jazz came from
a kind of music
called ragtime.

African Americans from New Orleans created jazz.

People often danced to jazz in the 1930s.

Jazz singing sometimes sounds like talking.

Jazz singers often sing out of time with the beat.

Jazz songs are often about love and friendship.

Some jazz singers sing sounds instead of words.

Jazz can be played on many different instruments. Some jazz musicians play the trumpet.

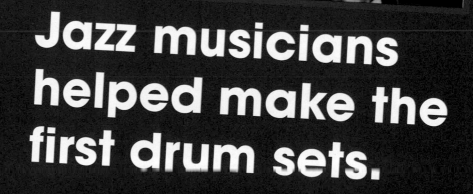

Jazz musicians helped make the first drum sets.

I like to play jazz with my friends. We never play a song the same way twice.

I learn to be part of a team when I play jazz in a band.

Jazz artists often play together at festivals. New Orleans holds a jazz festival each year.

More than 400,000 people go to New Orleans Jazz Fest each year.

I love jazz music. Playing music helps me learn new things.

JAZZ FACTS

These pages provide detailed information that expands on the interesting facts found in the book. They are intended to be used by adults as a learning support to help young readers round out their knowledge of each musical genre featured in the *I Love Music* series.

Pages 4–5

I love music. My favorite kind of music is jazz. Music is the name given to sounds made with voices or musical instruments and put together in a way that conveys emotion. People use music to express themselves. Jazz is a musical style played around the world. It is characterized by off-beat rhythms that produce a loose, "swinging" feel to the music. Jazz is known for its use of improvisation, which allows artists to make their songs more personal.

Pages 6–7

Jazz music came from Africa and Europe. African Americans brought to North America as slaves struggled to hold on to parts of their African culture. Jazz came about as a result of introducing West African rhythms and musical structures to traditional European instruments and harmonies. The most obvious forerunner to jazz was ragtime. Ragtime first popularized the off-beat rhythm that later came to define jazz.

Pages 8–9

African Americans from New Orleans created jazz. Musicians in New Orleans, Louisiana, blended several genres to create jazz. Musical elements from blues, ragtime, gospel choirs, opera, and traditional African drumming all came together to create jazz. Swing dancing became the national dance of the United States in the 1930s, largely due to the swinging jazz music played by big bands.

Pages 10–11

Jazz singing sometimes sounds like talking. Jazz singers often sing in the same pitch as their speaking voice. In this way, jazz singing veers closer to speech than more traditional forms of singing. In jazz, singers may stress different words or syllables, or even change notes to make the songs their own. Jazz singers help create a swinging feel to the music by stressing off-beat notes.

Pages 12–13

Jazz songs are often about love and friendship. Jazz music may have vocals, or it may be entirely instrumental. The lyrics of vocal jazz songs express the artists' feelings on a wide range of topics. Jazz singers are more known for an improvised, wordless style of singing called scat. In this style, the singer uses his or her voice like an instrument to produce melodies made up of nonsensical syllables.

Pages 14–15

Jazz can be played on many different instruments. Jazz was first played on the instruments available to African Americans in the early 1900s. These included the cornet, clarinet, trombone, tuba, piano, acoustic bass, and drums. Over the years, this list grew to include instruments from a range of other musical styles. In the 1930s and 1940s, some jazz bands featured upwards of 17 members, and were known as "big bands."

Pages 16–17

I like to play jazz with my friends. Playing music with others helps teach children cooperation, teamwork, and how to achieve goals. Children who regularly play music tend to have more confidence and get along better with others. Some students learn better in groups because they do not feel the pressure of having to learn on their own.

Pages 18–19

Jazz artists often play together at jazz festivals. The New Orleans Jazz and Heritage Festival is considered one of the world's greatest cultural events. Thousands of musicians perform at the 10-day festival each year. Since its inception in 1970, the festival has featured both local and international jazz legends, such as Fats Domino, Miles Davis, and Dizzy Gillespie.

Pages 20–21

I love jazz music. Playing music helps me learn new things. Recent studies suggest that learning and practicing music can be beneficial to a child's ability to learn. Among these benefits are improved motor skills and dexterity, increased test scores, and even raised Intelligence Quotient, or IQ, scores. Learning music at an early age has also been shown to aid in language development, and to improve reading and listening skills.

KEY WORDS

Research has shown that as much as 65 percent of all written material published in English is made up of 300 words. These 300 words cannot be taught using pictures or learned by sounding them out. They must be recognized by sight. This book contains 54 common sight words to help young readers improve their reading fluency and comprehension. This book also teaches young readers several important content words. These words are paired with pictures to aid in learning and improve understanding.

Page	Sight Words First Appearance
4	I, is, kind, my, of
5	began, in, states, the
6	and, came, from
7	a
8	Americans
9	often, people, to
10	like, sometimes, sounds
11	out, time, with
12	about, are, songs
13	some, words
14	be, can, different, many, on, play
15	first, make
16	never, same, way, we
17	learn, part, when
18	at, each, together, year
19	go, more, than
21	helps, me, new, things

Page	Content Words First Appearance
4	jazz, music
5	United States
6	Africa, Europe
7	ragtime
8	African Americans, New Orleans
10	singing
11	beat
12	friendship, love
14	instruments, musicians, trumpet
15	drum sets
16	friends
17	band, team
18	artists, festivals
19	New Orleans Jazz Fest

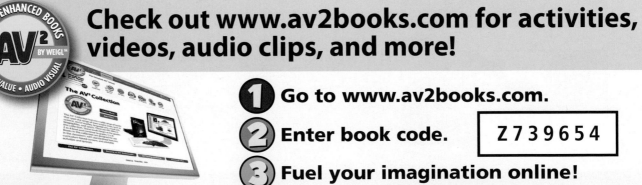